CONNECT MINDFULNESS, PURPOSE, AND PERSONAL FINANCE

10 Weeks of Self-ish Financial Wellness Transformation

Mindfulness + Purpose + Personal Finance

Author Ramat Oyetunji

We are proud to support Girls First by donating 50% of our journal net proceeds in 2024.
www.girlsfirst.org

Tinu Publishing LLC
121 N Bethlehem Pike #121
Suite 60
Spring House, PA 19447

ISBN 978-0-9863204-9-1 Paperback Print

What's Your Vibe?

Introduction

Do you want more balance, purpose, and harmony in your financial decisions and actions? Perhaps you're feeling dissatisfied, overwhelmed, or uninspired and looking to align your finances with your values for a more holistic financial wellness experience.

In today's environment of economic highs and lows, financial wellness is often associated with a high salary, high net worth, or other financial metrics. But true financial wellness goes beyond earning and accumulating money—it's about finding balance, purpose, and harmony in financial decisions and actions.

The 10-Week Guided Journal, based on The Self-ish Guide to Financial Wellness, taps into the power of journaling to help you explore and redefine financial wellness through practical steps and mindfulness practices. Discover strategies that help you uncover what truly matters to you and align your finances with your values and purpose.

Get started today to cultivate meaningful financial wellness that brings prosperity and harmony at any stage of your financial journey.

How to use the 10-Week Guided Journal

This journal is based on The Self-ish Guide to Financial Wellness and the Financial Wellness V.I.B.E.S™ philosophy. Summaries of the philosophy and the 9 strategies are provided in this journal.

Inside the pages of the journal, you will find guided prompts, actionable steps, empowering words and exercises, and plenty of space to reflect on your financial wellness each week.

With this journal, you can expect to:

- Apply mindfulness practices to uncover and connect with what truly matters to you.
- Incorporate mindfulness and purpose in your financial decisions.
- Learn strategies for managing money using a balanced approach.
- Take action to cultivate and attract more meaningful financial wellness.

Download a free copy of The Self-ish Guide to Financial Wellness using the QR code below for details, tips, and related stories on each strategy.

www.theselfishguide.com

About the Financial Wellness V.I.B.E.S™ Philosophy

What's your financial wellness vibe and what is it attracting? Your "vibe" is an energy you exude that acts like a magnet, attracting people and opportunities with similar energy as yours.

Your money beliefs, mindsets, attitudes, expectations, and actions create a financial wellness vibe that you project to others and attract from others.

The Financial Wellness V.I.B.E.S™ philosophy fosters five financial wellness beliefs or "vibes:" valuable, inspired, blessed, empowered, and satisfied.

Embracing these financial wellness vibes encourages you to make financial choices that are better aligned with what truly matters to you and enhance authentic financial wellness.

Follow Financial Wellness V.I.B.E.S™ on Instagram for insights, affirmations, tools, tips, templates, and more.

@financialwellnessvibes

The 5 Financial Wellness "Vibes"

V Valuable. You are valuable. Your talents, time, energy, and opinion are valuable. Know your value and expect to be valued.

I Inspired. You are open to inspiration and inspired to learn, live your best life, inspire others, and make the most of the resources and opportunities available.

B Blessed. You are blessed. Count your blessings, celebrate them, and believe with certainty that more blessings are coming your way.

E Empowered. You have the inner strength and will to advocate for yourself and act on any goal. You are open to new partnerships, opportunities, and experiences. When there isn't a seat at the table, you bring a chair!

S Satisfied. Your life isn't perfect and you are always striving to improve. Your satisfaction comes from knowing your financial decisions and actions align with your purpose and values.

The 9 Strategies

1 Cultivate an Abundance Mindset

What It Means: Cultivating an abundance mindset means focusing more on possibilities than limitations. It doesn't mean being wasteful, reckless, or oblivious. Instead, an abundance mindset looks for opportunities to thrive, even in challenging times. An abundance mindset also encourages generosity instead of a scarcity mindset.

How to Apply It: practice gratitude, visualize your dreams, examine things from different angles, welcome new experiences, offer and accept assistance, practice generosity, embrace shifting your perspective, and take a balanced approach to challenges.

2 Find True North

What It Means: Finding true north means discovering what truly matters to you and aligning your financial choices with those priorities. When you find your true north, it acts as an internal compass always seeking to align your decisions and actions with your values.

How to Apply It: explore things that inspire and motivate you, imagine your ideal life and think of all the elements that make it suitable for you, reflect on values that have always been a part of your life, assess your financial goals, and re-state them if they don't align to your true north.

The 9 Strategies

3 Know Your Worth

What It Means: Knowing your worth means acknowledging and recognizing your skills and contributions are valuable. When you know your worth, you can better appreciate the value you provide, communicate your value to others, and are less likely to make decisions that diminish your worth.

How to Apply It: evaluate your skills in detail—tangible and non-tangible—and compare them to similar skills in demand, reflect on the tasks you perform and the cost in terms of time, energy, and money and intangibles such as fulfillment; learn to set boundaries to protect and communicate your value.

4 Simplify and Get Rid of Clutter

What It Means: Getting rid of clutter means removing physical, mental, and emotional situations that create chaos and cause stress. Getting rid of financial clutter improves financial clarity, makes aligning with your purpose easier, and paves the way for more positive financial experiences and results.

How to Apply It: close or consolidate accounts, set a frequency for reviewing financial records, set up a system for financial record-keeping, go paperless, automate bill payments, and address financial mistakes holding you back.

The 9 Strategies

5 Say "No" More Often

What It Means: Saying "no" more often is not mean or selfish. It's about becoming more strategic and spending your time, energy, and money in ways that align with what matters to you. Saying "no" is easier said than done, but it can help prevent burnout, reduce stress, and leave you in a stronger position to help others. Learning when to say "no" can improve your financial and overall wellness.

How to Apply It: explore setting boundaries and find the ones that feel right, budget specific amounts of time and money for causes and obligations that are important to you, and practice saying "no" by starting with small matters.

6 Fill Your Buckets

What It Means: Filling your buckets means prioritizing financial resources to support what matters to you and planning to maintain the right level for each bucket (filling your buckets). It is a practical, balanced way of managing your finances while aligning with your purpose and values. There are five financial wellness buckets: needs, wants, obligations to others, self-care/growth, and causes/special interests.

How to Apply It: define items and fill level for each bucket, align your current spending to your determined fill level, and monitor each bucket for improvement.

The 9 Strategies

Fill Your Buckets

There are five financial wellness buckets:

- Needs
- Wants
- Obligations to Others
- Self-Care/Growth
- Causes/Special Interests

What items belong in each bucket? What is the right fill level for you? Which buckets have been neglected?

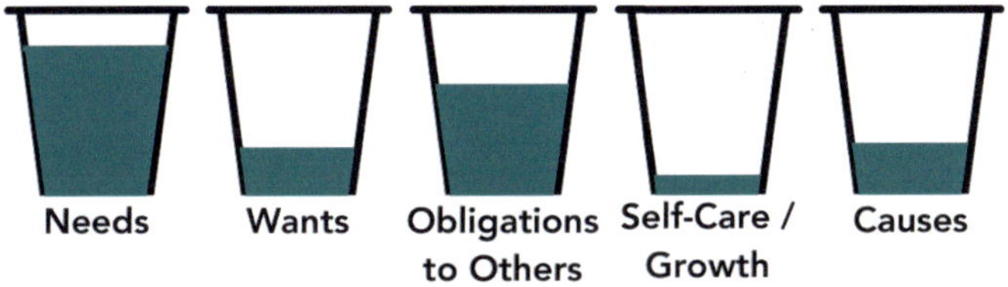

Follow Financial Wellness V.I.B.E.S™ on Instagram for additional insights, tools, and tips on filling your financial wellness buckets.

@financialwellnessvibes

The 9 Strategies

7 Enjoy the Journey

What It Means: Enjoying the journey means appreciating the experiences that have brought you this far, celebrating your progress, not comparing your journey to others, and looking forward to future success. Being present and expressing gratitude for your financial situation—imperfect as it may be!—is a big part of experiencing authentic financial wellness.

How to Apply It: Set bite-sized goals with clear milestones that allow you to track your progress and celebrate often. Share your success with others and make a point to celebrate theirs as well.

8 Embrace Lifelong Learning

What It Means: Lifelong learning means staying curious, expanding your knowledge, and being open to new opportunities. Becoming a lifelong learner helps you stay up-to-date and feel empowered with financial decisions. It adds a layer of security and growth to your financial wellness.

How to Apply It: prioritize time to expand your knowledge on financial topics, follow relevant accounts on social media, listen to podcasts, watch videos or read articles, and set goals to share and apply what you learned.

The 9 Strategies

9 Make It Routine

What It Means: Making it routine means streamlining, automating, and setting schedules for financial tasks and decisions. Making it routine makes it easier to complete tasks on time, anticipate changes, and adjust quickly. It also helps reduce financial anxiety and stress, creating more positive financial experiences.

How to Apply It: list financial tasks and decisions, identify recurring tasks suitable for automation, schedule financial activities and decision-making on your calendar, celebrate financial anniversaries, and pair up with a partner to encourage and support you.

Download the ebook.
The Self-ish Guide to Financial Wellness

www.theselfishguide.com

Begin Your Self-ish Financial Wellness Transformation!

Mindfulness + Purpose + Personal Finance

Financial Wellness Check in!

Before you begin, check in on your financial wellness

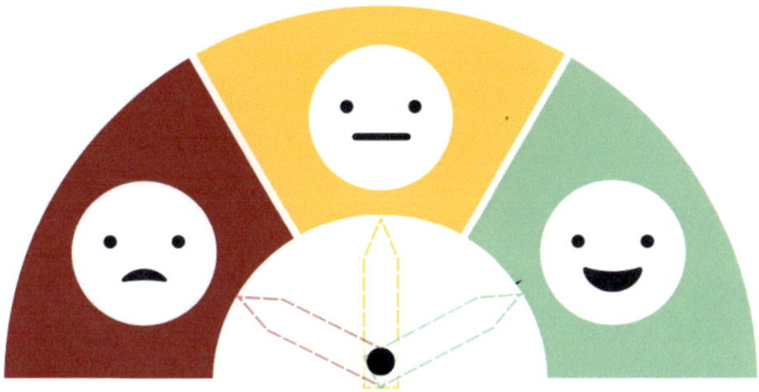

Use a pen or pencil to outline and fill the pointer that best describes your financial wellness

Financial Wellness Reflection

How well do your finances align with what matter most to you?

Valuable

You are valuable. Your talents, time, energy, and opinion are valuable.

WEEK 1

This Week's Financial Wellness Vibe:

- [x] **Valuable**
- [ ] **Inspired**
- [ ] **Blessed**
- [ ] **Empowered**
- [ ] **Satisfied**

Write two ways you will display this vibe to the world this week

When was the last time you reflected on the different ways you bring value to any table?

WEEK 1

Write a positive self-talk or affirmation to help you exude the "I'm valuable" vibe.

cut along the dotted line below and place your heart in a visible place for motivation

Unlock Strategy #1: Cultivate Abundance

When I think of cultivating abundance, I am most excited about ...

Suggested Actions for Unlocking Strategy #1: Cultivate Abundance

Get additional actions from The Self-ish Guide to Financial Wellness

- [ ] **Visualize**
  Imagine abundance in your life. Describe what that looks and feels like.

  What are the gaps compared to your current life? What role does finances play?

- [ ] **Reframe Challenges**
  Write down your biggest financial challenge. Reframe it as an opportunity.

  What actions do you need to take? Whose help or support do you need?

- [ ] **Practice Generosity**
  Write down a resource you own (time, talent, treasure) and will make available to others.

  Who could benefit from your generosity? How frequently will you make this resource available?

WEEK 1

This week's Financial Wellness Strategy:

- [x] Abundance
- [ ] Get Rid of Clutter
- [ ] Enjoy the Journey
- [ ] True North
- [ ] Say "No" More Often
- [ ] Lifelong Learner
- [ ] Know Your Worth
- [ ] Fill Your Buckets
- [ ] Make It Routine

The one action I will take this week to cultivate abundance is ...

WEEK 1

Reflection on my actions this week to cultivate abundance

Your Financial Wellness Buckets

What is one thing you will do this week to improve one of your financial wellness buckets?

Inspired

You are inspired to learn, take action, and make the most of resources and opportunities.

WEEK 2

This Week's Financial Wellness Vibe:

☐ Valuable ☑ Inspired ☐ Blessed ☐ Empowered ☐ Satisfied

Write two ways you will display this vibe to the world this week

When was the last time you reflected on your openness to inspiration?

WEEK 2

Write a positive self-talk or affirmation to help you exude the "I'm inspired" vibe.

cut along the dotted line below and place your heart in a visible place for motivation

Unlock Strategy #2: Find True North

When I think of finding True North, I am most excited about ...

Suggested Actions for Unlocking Strategy #2: Align to True North

Get additional actions from The Self-ish Guide to Financial Wellness

- [ ] **Self Reflection**
  List the situations and activities that bring you joy, fulfillment, and a sense of purpose.

- [ ] **Reality Check**
  Review your spending for the previous 1-3 months.

  How well are your finances aligned with the things on your list that bring you joy, fulfillment and purpose?

- [ ] **Become Intentional**
  Identify one thing on your budget or spending that doesn't align with your list and make a plan to gradually eliminate it.

  Identify one thing on your list that isn't in your budget or spending and make a plan to include it.

  Repeat this process as often as you need.

WEEK 2

This week's Financial Wellness Strategy:

☐ Abundance	☐ Get Rid of Clutter	☐ Enjoy the Journey
☑ True North	☐ Say "No" More Often	☐ Lifelong Learner
☐ Know Your Worth	☐ Fill Your Buckets	☐ Make It Routine

The one action I will take this week to find True North is ...

WEEK 2

Reflection on my actions this week to find True North

Your Financial Wellness Buckets

What is one thing you will do this week to improve one of your financial wellness buckets?

Blessed

You are blessed. Count your blessings, celebrate them, and look for ways to bless others.

WEEK 3

This Week's Financial Wellness Vibe:

☐ **Valuable** ☐ **Inspired** ☑ **Blessed** ☐ **Empowered** ☐ **Satisfied**

Write two ways you will display this vibe to the world this week

When was the last time you reflected on all the ways you are blessed?

WEEK 3

Write a positive self-talk or affirmation to help you exude the "I'm blessed" vibe.

cut along the dotted line below and place your heart in a visible place for motivation

Unlock Strategy #3: Know Your Worth

When I think of knowing my worth, I am most excited about ...

Suggested Actions for Unlocking Strategy #3: Know Your Worth

Get additional actions from The Self-ish Guide to Financial Wellness

- [ ] **Who You Are**
  Reflect on your unique skills, talents, and experiences. List them and note the impact they have had.

  What are the ripple effects of your talent, time, and energy?

- [ ] **Get the Market Rate**
  Compare your skills, talents, and experience with the current rates being offered for similar portfolios of work.

  How well does your current compensation reflect your market value? Is your compensation worth the price you pay in health, time, and energy?

- [ ] **Set Clear Boundaries**
  Set boundaries that reflect your value. Identify work that isn't valued, unpaid, or doesn't align with the talents you bring to the table.

  What steps will you take to reduce or eliminate this list?

This week's Financial Wellness Strategy:

- [ ] Abundance
- [ ] True North
- [x] Know Your Worth
- [ ] Get Rid of Clutter
- [ ] Say "No" More Often
- [ ] Fill Your Buckets
- [ ] Enjoy the Journey
- [ ] Lifelong Learner
- [ ] Make It Routine

The one action I will take this week to know my worth is ...

WEEK 3

Reflection on my actions this week to know my worth

Your Financial Wellness Buckets

What is one thing you will do this week to improve one of your financial wellness buckets?

Empowered

You are empowered. You have the inner strength to achieve your goals and embrace new opportunities.

WEEK 4

This Week's Financial Wellness Vibe:

☐ Valuable ☐ Inspired ☐ Blessed ☑ Empowered ☐ Satisfied

Write two ways you will display this vibe to the world this week

When was the last time you reflected on how your inner strength empowers you?

WEEK 4

Write a positive self-talk or affirmation to help you exude the "I'm empowered" vibe.

cut along the dotted line below and place your heart in a visible place for motivation

Unlock Strategy #4: Simplify & De-Clutter

When I think of simplifying and getting rid of clutter, I am most excited about ...

Suggested Actions for Unlocking Strategy #4: Get Rid of Clutter

Get additional actions from The Self-ish Guide to Financial Wellness

☐ **Physical Clutter**
Set a scheduled day and time to tackle financial clutter. Have a specific goal. Example: set a day to sort and organize bills and a day for financial paperwork.

How will you stick to your plan? Can you enlist the help of an accountability partner or pair your decluttering activity with another activity you enjoy e.g. watching a show?

☐ **Mental Clutter**
Get your financial goals and worries out of your head. Write them down, prioritize them, and track your progress at a frequency that works for you.

☐ **Emotional Clutter**
Practice self-compassion and kindness towards yourself concerning financial mistakes or decisions you regret. Consider these mistakes lessons to learn from, and reflect on ways to avoid repeating them.

WEEK 4

This week's Financial Wellness Strategy:

- [ ] Abundance
- [x] Get Rid of Clutter
- [ ] Enjoy the Journey
- [ ] True North
- [ ] Say "No" More Often
- [ ] Lifelong Learner
- [ ] Know Your Worth
- [ ] Fill Your Buckets
- [ ] Make It Routine

The one action I will take this week to simplify and get rid of clutter is ...

WEEK 4

Reflection on my actions this week to simplify and de-clutter

Your Financial Wellness Buckets

What is one thing you will do this week to improve one of your financial wellness buckets?

Satisfied.

You feel satisfied. Your life isn't perfect but you are at peace with your financial decisions and actions.

WEEK 5

This Week's Financial Wellness Vibe:

☐ **Valuable** ☐ **Inspired** ☐ **Blessed** ☐ **Empowered** ☑ **Satisfied**

Write two ways you will display this vibe to the world this week

When was the last time you reflected on the satisfaction of making a decision that aligned with your values?

WEEK 5

Write a positive self-talk or affirmation to help you exude the "I'm satisfied" vibe.

cut along the dotted line below and place your heart in a visible place for motivation

Unlock Strategy #5: Say "NO" More Often

When I think of saying "no" more often, I am most excited about ...

Suggested Actions for Unlocking Strategy #5: Say "NO" More Often

Get additional actions from The Self-ish Guide to Financial Wellness

☐ **Check Yourself**
Reflect on your recent obligations, spending, or energy drains. Were any of them done reluctantly? Did you want to say "no" but instead said "yes?"

Check in with yourself frequently to ensure you honor the boundaries you set and release any guilt associated with saying "no."

☐ **Practice Makes Perfect**
Think of a time you spent time or money you didn't have or pursued an opportunity that wasn't right just because you felt "you should."

How will you say "no" the next time you face a similar scenario? Write down a few things you could do. Repeat this exercise often.

☐ **Celebrate Saying "No"**
Acknowledge and celebrate each time you successfully say no, reinforcing your desire to become more intentional and aligned with what matters most to you.

WEEK 5

This week's Financial Wellness Strategy:

- [ ] **Abundance**
- [ ] **Get Rid of Clutter**
- [ ] **Enjoy the Journey**
- [ ] **True North**
- [x] **Say "No" More Often**
- [ ] **Lifelong Learner**
- [ ] **Know Your Worth**
- [ ] **Fill Your Buckets**
- [ ] **Make It Routine**

The one action I will take this week to say "no" more often is ...

WEEK 5

Reflection on my actions this week to say "no" more often

Your Financial Wellness Buckets

What is one thing you will do this week to improve one of your financial wellness buckets?

Financial Wellness Check in!

You're amazing! You've completed 5 weeks!
Check in on your financial wellness ...

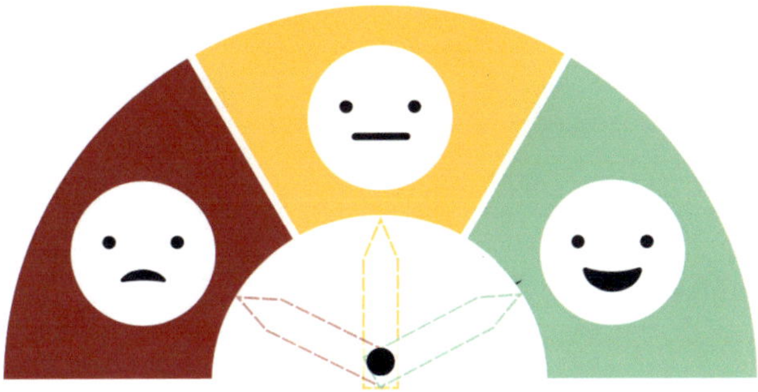

Use a pen or pencil to outline and fill the pointer that best describes your financial wellness

Financial Wellness Reflection

Valuable

*You are valuable.
Recognize and
appreciate your value.
Expect to be valued.*

WEEK 6

This Week's Financial Wellness Vibe:

- [x] **Valuable**
- [ ] **Inspired**
- [ ] **Blessed**
- [ ] **Empowered**
- [ ] **Satisfied**

Write two ways you will display this vibe to the world this week

When was the last time you reflected on how your value is utilized, acknowledged, appreciated, and rewarded?

WEEK 6

Write a positive self-talk or affirmation to help you exude the "I'm valuable" vibe.

cut along the dotted line below and place your heart in a visible place for motivation

Unlock Strategy #6: Fill Your Buckets

When I think of filling my buckets, I am most excited about ...

Suggested Actions for Unlocking Strategy #6: Fill Your Buckets

Get additional actions from The Self-ish Guide to Financial Wellness

☐ **First, Convince Yourself!**
Does the thought of filling your financial wellness buckets make you feel selfish? Remember that caring for yourself puts you in a stronger position to weather storms and help others.

☐ **Determine What Goes In Each Bucket**
Reflect on your true north and determine the items you want in each bucket. Compare your recent spending and budget items to your list.

Are there any items that don't belong? Now is a great time to become intentional with your spending, budget, and goals.

☐ **The Right Fill Level For You**
Each bucket will have a different fill level that feels right to you. Experiment with fill levels to discover what works best for you.

WEEK 6

This week's Financial Wellness Strategy:

- [ ] Abundance
- [ ] Get Rid of Clutter
- [ ] Enjoy the Journey
- [ ] True North
- [ ] Say "No" More Often
- [ ] Lifelong Learner
- [ ] Know Your Worth
- [x] Fill Your Buckets
- [ ] Make It Routine

The one action I will take this week to fill my buckets is ...

WEEK 6

Reflection on my actions this week to fill my buckets

Your Financial Wellness Buckets

What is one thing you will do this week to improve one of your financial wellness buckets?

Inspired

You inspire others with your actions and willingness to share resources and lift others.

WEEK 7

This Week's Financial Wellness Vibe:

☐ **Valuable** ☑ **Inspired** ☐ **Blessed** ☐ **Empowered** ☐ **Satisfied**

Write two ways you will display this vibe to the world this week

When was the last time you reflected on how well you inspire others?

WEEK 7

Write a positive self-talk or affirmation to help you exude the "I'm inspired" vibe.

cut along the dotted line below and place your heart in a visible place for motivation

Unlock Strategy #7: Enjoy the Journey

When I think of enjoying the journey, I am most excited about ...

Suggested Actions for Unlocking Strategy #7: Enjoy the Journey

Get additional actions from The Self-ish Guide to Financial Wellness

☐ **Practice Gratitude. Don't Compare**
Reflect on three things you are grateful for from your financial journey. Express gratitude for the blessings, experiences, challenges, and learnings your financial journey has provided. Be intentional about not comparing your journey to anyone else's. Your journey is unique!

☐ **Don't Sweat the Small Stuff**
Be intentional about learning and moving on from mistakes. List the mistakes that still haunt you and reflect on what you would have done differently. Forgive yourself and permit yourself to move on.

☐ **Celebrate All Wins - Big and Small**
Make celebrating wins part of your routine. Each time you hit a new milestone, learn something new, or take action, celebrate it! Make a big deal of it.

Create financial anniversaries and find ways to commemorate them.

WEEK 7

This week's Financial Wellness Strategy:

- [ ] **Abundance**
- [ ] **Get Rid of Clutter**
- [x] **Enjoy the Journey**
- [ ] **True North**
- [ ] **Say "No" More Often**
- [ ] **Lifelong Learner**
- [ ] **Know Your Worth**
- [ ] **Fill Your Buckets**
- [ ] **Make It Routine**

The one action I will take this week to enjoy the journey is ...

WEEK 7

Reflection on my actions this week to enjoy the journey

Your Financial Wellness Buckets

What is one thing you will do this week to improve one of your financial wellness buckets?

Blessed

You are blessed. Believe with certainty that more blessings are coming your way.

WEEK 8

This Week's Financial Wellness Vibe:

☐ Valuable ☐ Inspired ☑ Blessed ☐ Empowered ☐ Satisfied

Write two ways you will display this vibe to the world this week

When was the last time you reflected on all the ways you can bless others?

WEEK 8

Write a positive self-talk or affirmation to help you exude the "I'm blessed" vibe.

cut along the dotted line below and place your heart in a visible place for motivation

Unlock Strategy #8: Become a Lifelong Learner

When I think of becoming a lifelong learner, I am most excited about ...

Suggested Actions for Unlocking Strategy #8: Become a Lifelong Learner

Get additional actions from The Self-ish Guide to Financial Wellness

- [ ] **Keep It Simple**
  Commit to learning something every week and choose the most convenient medium for you. For example, if you prefer reading articles to watching videos, commit to reading more personal finance articles or blog posts.

- [ ] **Talk About It and Share**
  Challenge yourself to speak more openly about finances and be willing to share what you learn. It will help deepen your understanding of the topic, help others learn, and open you to learning from others.

- [ ] **Apply It!**
  Apply what you learn and uncover what works or doesn't work for you. The more you practice, the more fluent you become in the things you are learning.

WEEK 8

This week's Financial Wellness Strategy:

- [ ] Abundance
- [ ] Get Rid of Clutter
- [ ] Enjoy the Journey
- [ ] True North
- [ ] Say "No" More Often
- [x] Lifelong Learner
- [ ] Know Your Worth
- [ ] Fill Your Buckets
- [ ] Make It Routine

The one action I will take this week to become a lifelong learner is ...

WEEK 8

Reflection on my actions this week to become a lifelong learner

Your Financial Wellness Buckets

What is one thing you will do this week to improve one of your financial wellness buckets?

Empowered

You are empowered to advocate for what is right for you and aligns with your purpose.

WEEK 9

This Week's Financial Wellness Vibe:

☐ Valuable ☐ Inspired ☐ Blessed ☑ Empowered ☐ Satisfied

Write two ways you will display this vibe to the world this week

When was the last time you advocated for yourself?

WEEK 9

Write a positive self-talk or affirmation to help you exude the "I'm empowered" vibe.

cut along the dotted line below and place your heart in a visible place for motivation

Unlock Strategy #9: Make It Routine

When I think of making it routine, I am most excited about ...

Suggested Actions for Unlocking Strategy #9: Make It Routine

Get additional actions from The Self-ish Guide to Financial Wellness

- [ ] **Automate**
  Make a list of your typical financial tasks and decisions such as paying bills.

  Which ones can you automate? How often will you review them for changes?

- [ ] **Pair With Existing Routines**
  Identify your current routines and look for opportunities to incorporate financial tasks or mindfulness habits that foster positive financial associations.

  Examples: daily affirmations and intention setting in the shower to start the day, completing financial tasks while watching a show, expressing gratitude for your financial situation at bedtime, etc.

- [ ] **Make It a "Thing"**
  Partner with a friend or family member who can provide encouragement and accountability and make discussing or reviewing finances the "thing" you do together.

  What frequency would you meet? How would you make it more fun?

WEEK 9

This week's Financial Wellness Strategy:

- [ ] **Abundance**
- [ ] **Get Rid of Clutter**
- [ ] **Enjoy the Journey**
- [ ] **True North**
- [ ] **Say "No" More Often**
- [ ] **Lifelong Learner**
- [ ] **Know Your Worth**
- [ ] **Fill Your Buckets**
- [x] **Make It Routine**

The one action I will take this week to make it routine is ...

WEEK 9

Reflection on my actions this week to make it routine

Your Financial Wellness Buckets

What is one thing you will do this week to improve one of your financial wellness buckets?

Satisfied

You feel satisfied knowing you are making progress with every step you take.

WEEK 10

This Week's Financial Wellness Vibe:

☐ **Valuable** ☐ **Inspired** ☐ **Blessed** ☐ **Empowered** ☑ **Satisfied**

Write two ways you will display this vibe to the world this week

When was the last time you reflected on the satisfaction you get from small financial wins?

WEEK 10

Write a positive self-talk or affirmation to help you exude the "I'm satisfied" vibe.

cut along the dotted line below and place your heart in a visible place for motivation

Your Financial Wellness Buckets

What is one thing you will do this week to improve one of your financial wellness buckets?

Financial Wellness Check in!

Congrats, you made it to the end! Check in on your financial wellness ...

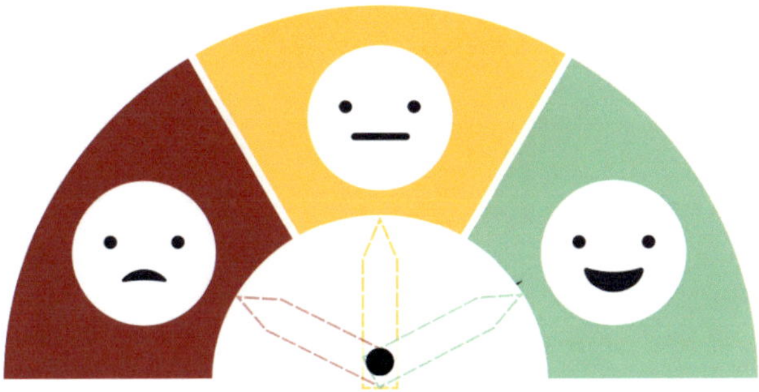

Use a pen or pencil to outline and fill the pointer that best describes your financial wellness

Financial Wellness Reflection

Follow-up items and final thoughts from weeks 1 – 10

Follow-up items from week 1

Follow-up items from week 1

WEEK 2

Follow-up items from week 2

Follow-up items from week 2

WEEK 3

Follow-up items from week 3

Follow-up items from week 3

Follow-up items from week 4

Follow-up items from week 4

Follow-up items from week 5

Follow-up items from week 5

Follow-up items from week 6

Follow-up items from week 6

Follow-up items from week 7

WEEK 7

Follow-up items from week 7

Follow-up items from week 8

Follow-up items from week 8

Follow-up items from week 9

Follow-up items from week 9

Follow-up items from week 10

Follow-up items from week 10

We want to hear about your self-ish financial wellness journey! Share your journey with us on Instagram.

@financialwellnessvibes

Made in the USA
Monee, IL
12 September 2026

62981021R00086